W9-ABT-021

Bannockburn School Dist. 106
2165 Telegraph Road
Bannockburn, Illinois 60015

Yellow Umbrella Books are published by Capstone Press
151 Good Counsel Drive, P.O. Box 669, Mankato, Minnesota 56002
www.capstonepress.com

Library of Congress Cataloging-in-Publication Data
Shepard, Daniel.
All kinds of farms / by Daniel Shepard.
p. cm.
Summary: Simple text and photographs introduce crops that grow in a variety of locations and climates.
ISBN-13: 978-0-7368-2912-0 (hardcover)
ISBN-10: 0-7368-2912-1 (hardcover)
ISBN-13: 978-0-7368-2871-0 (softcover)
ISBN-10: 0-7368-2871-0 (softcover)
1. Fruit—Juvenile literature. 2. Vegetables—Juvenile literature. 3. Farms—Juvenile literature. [1. Crops. 2. Farms.] I. Title.
SB357.2.S54 2004
630—dc21   2003009322

Editorial Credits
Editorial Director: Mary Lindeen
Editor: Jennifer VanVoorst
Photo Researcher: Wanda Winch
Developer: Raindrop Publishing

Photo Credits
Cover: Royalty-Free/Corbis; Title Page: PhotoLink/PhotoDisc; Page 2: Royalty Free/Corbis; Page 3: Corel; Page 4: Ron Colbroth/Folio, Inc.; Page 5: Gerald and Buff Corsi/Visuals Unlimited; Page 6: T. O'Keefe/PhotoLink/PhotoDisc; Page 7: PhotoLink/PhotoDisc; Page 8: Royalty-Free/Corbis; Page 9: New York Apple Association; Page 10: DigitalVision; Page 11: Corel; Page 12: Bob Rashid/Brand X Pictures; Page 13: DigitalVision; Page 14: James H. Karales/USDA; Page 15: Emma Lee/Life File/PhotoDisc; Page 16: Doug Menuez/PhotoDisc

All Kinds of Farms

by Daniel Shepard

Consultant: Leesa Witt, Director of Education
National Farmers Union

Yellow Umbrella Books

an imprint of Capstone Press
Mankato, Minnesota

There are many different
kinds of farms. Some farms
grow grains.

This rice farm is called a paddy.
Rice is a grain.

Some farms grow fruit.

The oranges on this farm are ready to be picked.

Some farms are big.
This big farm grows corn.

Other farms are small. This
small farm grows tomatoes.

Some farms are in hot places.
Pineapples need the hot sun
to grow.

This banana farm is in a hot place, too. It is in a rain forest.

Other farms are in cool places. Pumpkins grow best in cool weather.

Apples on this farm need cool weather, too.

The grapes on this farm are
ready for harvest.

The cranberries on this farm
are ready for harvest, too.

This is a potato farm. Where
are the potatoes? They grow
under the ground!

Some farms even grow flowers!

There are all kinds of farms!

Words to Know/Index

Word Count: 146
Early-Intervention Level: 11